Rookie biographies

Betsy Ross

By Wil Mara

Consultant
Nanci R. Vargus, EdD
Assistant Professor of Literacy
University of Indianapolis
Indianapolis, Indiana

Children's Press®
A Division of Scholastic Inc.
New York   Toronto   London   Auckland   Sydney
Mexico City   New Delhi   Hong Kong
Danbury, Connecticut

Designer: Herman Adler Design
Photo Researcher: Caroline Anderson
The photo on the cover shows Betsy Ross.

Library of Congress Cataloging-in-Publication Data

Mara, Wil.
  Betsy Ross / by Wil Mara.
      p. cm. — (Rookie biographies)
  Includes index.
    ISBN 0-516-25268-2 (lib. bdg.)   0-516-25369-7 (pbk.)
    1. Ross, Betsy, 1752–1836—Juvenile literature. 2. Revolutionaries—United
States—Biography—Juvenile literature. 3. United States—History—Revolution,
1775–1783—Flags—Juvenile literature. 4. Flags—United States—History—
18th century—Juvenile literature. I. Title. II. Rookie biography.
  E302.6.R77M37 2005
  973.'092—dc22   2005004028

CHILDREN'S PRESS, and ROOKIE BIOGRAPHIES®, and associated
logos are trademarks and/or registered trademarks of Scholastic Library
Publishing. SCHOLASTIC and associated logos are trademarks and/or
registered trademarks of Scholastic Inc.
6 7 8 9 10 R 14 13 12 11   62

Betsy Ross was one of the first female heroes in American history.

She was born in Philadelphia, Pennsylvania, on January 1, 1752.

Her name was Elizabeth Griscom. "Betsy" was her nickname.

This is what Philadelphia looked like around the time Betsy was born.

6

Betsy learned how to sew in school. She became very good at it.

She left school while she was still a teenager. She got a job sewing in a shop in Philadelphia.

She made clothes, blankets, and other things.

This is one of the shops where Betsy worked.

John Ross also worked at the shop where he met Betsy.

10

She met a man named John Ross at this shop. They got married in 1773. She changed her name to Betsy Ross.

There is a famous story about Betsy Ross. It says three men came to visit her and asked her to make a flag.

14

One of the men was George Washington. He would later become America's first president.

In the 1770s, America was at war with Great Britain.

Great Britain ruled America at that time. Most Americans, however, wanted to live free of Great Britain's control.

America had to have its own flag. It was one way to show that America was its own country.

Ross made a flag that had 13 stripes. The stripes were red and white.

The flag also had a blue rectangle in one corner. The blue rectangle had 13 stars inside.

Ross used 13 stars because there were 13 colonies in America in 1776. These colonies later became states.

America has added 37 more states since then!

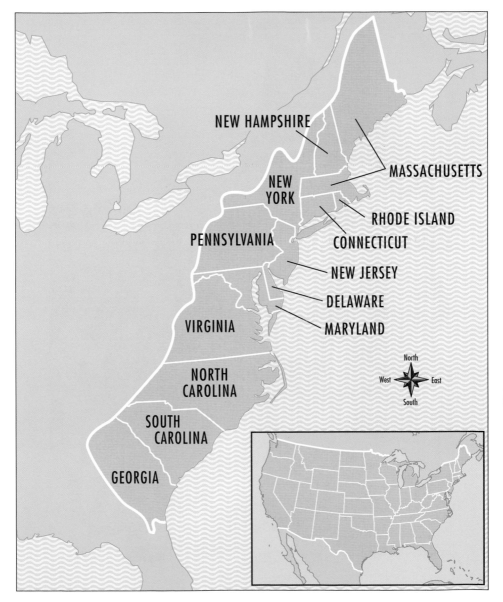

NEW HAMPSHIRE

MASSACHUSETTS

NEW YORK

RHODE ISLAND

CONNECTICUT

PENNSYLVANIA

NEW JERSEY

DELAWARE

MARYLAND

VIRGINIA

North
West East
South

NORTH CAROLINA

SOUTH CAROLINA

GEORGIA

21

Washington loved the new flag. He and the other leaders of America accepted it as the symbol of their country's independence.

Ross did more for America than sew flags.

She gave food and water to soldiers. She also took care of soldiers who were hurt.

Some historians wonder if Betsy Ross really did make the first American flag.

No one knows for sure.

We do know that Betsy Ross was a great American.

You can visit the Betsy Ross House in Philadelphia, Pennsylvania.

There you will learn more about Betsy Ross and the American flag.

Words You Know

Betsy Ross

Betsy Ross House

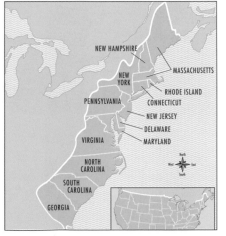

colonies

flag

George Washington

Philadelphia

sewing

war

Index

About the Author

Wil Mara has written more than seventy books. He has written both fiction and nonfiction, for both children and adults.

Photo Credits

Photographs © 2005: Art Resource, NY: 17, 31 bottom right; Corbis Images: 6, 26, 31 bottom left (Bettmann), 13 (Francis G. Mayer), 29, 30 top right (Lee Snider/Photo Images); Getty Images/Hulton Archive: 18, 25, 30 bottom right; Library of Congress: cover; Mary Evans Picture Library: 3, 30 top left; North Wind Picture Archives: 5, 9, 22, 31 top right; Superstock, Inc.: 14, 31 top left (Christie's Images), 10. Maps on 21, 30 bottom left by Bob Italiano